Busy Weekdays Recipes

Top 77 Recipes: *Energy Breakfast, Lunch Box, Immunity Boosting Smoothies, Meat, Salads, Sandwiches, Soups, Pre-Workout Meals and Snacks, Desserts*

Good Food for Successful People!

Tables of contents

Introduction

For many people cooks, preparing homemade meals after a long strenuous day at work is sometimes hard and even overwhelming. We all have nights when we don't feel like cooking anything complicated or simply don't have the energy to make elaborate meals that no one will eat. With so many commitments these days, convenience usually wins out over healthy most days of the week.

The 5 or less ingredient recipes in this cookbook will help you get delicious healthy meals on the table in an hour or less and will make your hectic day a little less stressful. A good recipe doesn't need a long list of ingredients to make it tasty and while preparing meals at home may seem hard at the beginning, you will soon realize you can throw together a healthy freinds dinner in the same amount of time you'd need to order a takeout.

With just five simple ingredients, you can have dinner, a snack or a meal on the table in no time flat. You don't need a huge pantry with shelves of ingredients to serve your family everything from super easy snacks and appetizers to scrumptious salads, suppers and delectable desserts. With a minimum of ingredients, a few basic cooking techniques and great recipes that let the natural tastes of the good food shine through, you're set to satisfy your family and guests with delicious recipes that will become favorite go-to solutions for every occasion.

Fast, Fast, Fast!

How would you like to be able to come home and have a fresh, hot and savory meal on the table in 30 minutes? It's easy to pull off dinner in a half hour when you use recipes that don't require a lot of preparation.

Simplicity and Planning

Not every recipe can be ready-to-eat in 30 minutes, but you certainly won't spend a lot of time preparing your meals.

If time is in short supply, preplan your day's menu. Prepare ingredients like chopped onions, peppers and celery in the morning before leaving for work.

You can even chop up batches of often-used fresh vegetables like celery and onion, package them in 1/2-cup servings in resealable snack bags and freeze. Then, you're ready anytime you need these ingredients for frying, baking or soups and stews. Refrigerated desserts and salads only take a few minutes to throw together in the morning. Refrigerate for the day and they're ready to serve when you get home in the evening. Many of these recipes can be assembled the night before and refrigerated. Then in the morning, just pop it in the oven and you have a hearty meal without the hassle.

1.Breakfast

During a busy morning, it's easy to let breakfast fall low in your list of priorities, but taking just a few minutes to prepare a healthy breakfast can really make a difference to the way you metabolize glucose, and control blood sugar, all day.

What you eat is important. Food is fuel for the body, so eating a nutritious breakfast means you'll have enough energy to burn, keeping you active and productive until lunchtime. And a healthy breakfast can set the tone for nutritious choices all day long. Fortunately, there are plenty of traditional breakfast foods that are delicious and are good for you. Using more fruits and vegetables for breakfast along with whole grains and lean meats, nuts and seeds, eggs and Greek yogurt is a safe and natural way to lose or maintain a healthy weight. Try these easy breakfast ideas to give your body the kick-start it needs.

Important!

Start each day with a glass of clean water. Just make a couple of sips - and you will feel how the body becomes more active and the feeling of drowsiness disappears!

Energy Boost to Start the Day

Everyone should start their day off right by eating as many vitamins and other nutrients as possible. The great thing about breakfast is there are so many common breakfast foods that can be considered super-foods because of their nutrition value:

- Eggs
- Whole grains
- Vitamin C

Sharper Focus

By eating breakfast every morning, you are able to be more focused and productive until it's time to refuel at lunch. But when you skip out on breakfast, it's hard not to think about anything except food, especially with a noisy stomach that needs to be fed.

Breakfast Helps Reduce Morning Crankiness

Feeling cranky during the morning is understandable - you probably wanted to stay in bed for a few extra winks, you don't feel like going to work, and what most people forget, you're starving! Imagine going without food for 8 to 12 hours during the day; you probably won't be the most approachable person in the office or classroom.

Allows You to Properly Portion Your Meals

You may not feel very hungry when you initially wake up, but eating a healthy, balanced breakfast can help you plan and portion out your meals for the rest of the day. That way, you won't be tempted to binge eat or snack unnecessarily, both of which are unhealthy habits that can lead you to ignore your nutrition by satisfying hunger cravings with fatty foods anytime you like.

Breakfast Can Be Nutritious and Delicious

Start the day off with a healthy and delicious meal. You can even indulge a bit with some crispy bacon, sausage links or pancakes. Just make sure to have something with a high nutritional value on the side like a slice of cantaloupe or a bowl of fresh strawberries.

For breakfast, you can add a cup of tea or coffee. But it is better to drink fruit juice or fresh. And coffee and tea will help you after lunch!

Crunchy Granola Wedges

Serves: 8 Calories: 279

Preparation Time: 35 minutes

Ingredients

- 1 cup rolled oats
- 1 cup wheat flakes
- 1 cup sunflower seeds or chopped nuts
- ½ cup honey
- 1 cup dried cranberries

Method

1. Preheat oven to 400F/205C.
2. Spread oats, wheat flakes and seeds (or nuts) on a baking sheet.
3. Bake until fragrant and starting to brown about 10 minutes.
4. Coat a 9-inch pie pan with cooking spray.
5. Cook ½ cup honey in a large saucepan over medium-high heat, without stirring, until large foamy bubbles form and it starts to darken at the edges, 2 to 4 minutes. (The bubbles will start out small and increase to about ¾ inch or larger when the honey's done.)
6. Immediately pour the toasted oat mixture into the honey, add cranberries and salt and stir until completely coated.
7. Quickly press the granola into the prepared pie pan using a heat-resistant spatula coated with cooking spray. Let cool for 30 minutes.
8. Cut into wedges and transfer to a wire rack to cool completely.

Quick Breakfast Taco

Serves: 1   Calories: 239

Preparation Time: 5 minutes

Ingredients

- 2 corn tortillas
- 1 tablespoon salsa
- 2 tablespoons shredded reduced-fat Cheddar cheese
- ½ cup liquid egg substitute, such as Egg Beaters
- Pinch of salt

Method

1. Top tortillas with salsa and cheese.
2. Heat in the microwave until the cheese is melted, about 30 seconds.
3. Meanwhile coat a small nonstick skillet with cooking spray.
4. Heat over medium heat, add egg substitute and cook, stirring, until the eggs are cooked through, about 90 seconds.
5. Divide the scrambled egg between the tacos.

Yankee Grits

Serves: 1 Calories: 336

Preparation Time: 5 minutes

Ingredients

- 1 cup low-fat milk or water
- 2 teaspoons pure maple syrup
- Pinch of salt
- ¼ cup quick-cooking grits
- 2 tablespoons raisins, dried cranberries or chopped dried fruit

Method

1. Bring milk (or water), syrup and salt to a boil in a small saucepan over high heat.
2. Slowly whisk in grits, reduce heat to medium-low, cover and cook, stirring occasionally, until thickened, 3 to 4 minutes.
3. Let stand for 1 minute.
4. Serve sprinkled with dried fruit.

Florentine Hash Skillet

Serves: 1   Calories: 226

Preparation Time: 7 minutes

Ingredients

- 1 teaspoon extra-virgin olive oil
- ½ cup frozen hash browns or precooked shredded potatoes
- ½ cup frozen chopped spinach
- 1 large egg
- Pinch of salt and pepper
- 2 tablespoons shredded sharp Cheddar cheese

Method

1. Heat oil in a small nonstick skillet over medium heat. Layer hash browns and spinach into the pan.
2. Crack egg on top and sprinkle with salt, pepper and cheese.
3. Cover, reduce heat to medium-low and cook until the hash browns are starting to brown on the bottom, the egg is set and the cheese is melted, 4 to 7 minutes.

Quick Coconut Macaroons

Serves: 1   Calories: 526

Cooking Time: 12 minutes

Ingredients

- 2/3 cup Wheat flour
- 5 1/2 cup Coconut meat
- 1/4 tsp Salt
- 1 cup Canned milk
- 2 tsp Vanilla extract

Directions

1. Preheat oven to 350F/180C. Line cookie sheets with parchment paper or aluminum foil.
2. In a large bowl, stir together the flour, coconut and salt. Stir in the sweetened condensed milk and vanilla using your hands until well blended.
3. Use an ice cream scoop to drop dough onto the prepared cookie sheets. Cookies should be about golf ball size.
4. Bake for 12 to 15 minutes in the preheated oven, until coconut is toasted.

Pasta with Tuna and Tomato Sauce

Serves: 4 Calories: 426

Cooking Time: 35 minutes

Ingredients

- 16 oz Pasta Corn, dry
- 2 can (15 oz)Tomatoes Crushed, canned
- 4 tbsp Butter Unsalted
- 1/2 cup Parmesan cheese Grated
- 6 oz Tuna Fish, light, canned in oil, drained solids
- 1/2 cup Ricotta cheese Whole milk
- 1 dash salt
- 1/4 cup Fresh Basil leaves, whole

Directions

1. Chop or tear fresh basil. Melt the butter in a medium pot on medium heat and add the can of tomatoes, including the juice. If you are using whole canned tomatoes (or fresh ones) crush them with your (clean) fingers as you put them in the pot. Simmer gently, partially covered, for 30 minutes.
2. Once the sauce is cooking, heat a large pot of well salted water to a strong boil. Add the shell pasta to the boiling water and cook at a vigorous boil, uncovered, until al dente, cooked through but still a bit firm to the bite, which is usually whatever the time specified on the pasta package minus about 2 minutes. Drain and set aside.
3. Pour off the excess oil from the tuna can and stir the tuna into the tomato sauce. Add the ricotta cheese, and add salt to taste. Turn off the heat. Mix the sauce with the pasta in a large bowl. Mix in the basil.
4. Pour the pasta into a 2 to 3-quart casserole dish and top with the parmesan cheese. Put under a hot broiler for 4-6 minutes, until the cheese is melted and lightly browned. Serve hot.

BBQ Chicken Burrito Bowls

Serves: 4 Calories: 603

Cooking Time: 25 minutes

Ingredients

- 2 half breast (fillet) Chicken breast
- 2 tsp Olive oil
- 1 tbsp Salt
- 1 tbsp Pepper
- 4 cup White rice
- 1/2 cup (8 fl oz) Barbecue sauce
- 1 15/17 cup Black beans
- 1 cup Corn
- 1 small Zucchini
- 1 cup, shredded Monterey cheese
- 2 large Scallions
- Avocados 1 fruit, without skin

Directions

1. Preheat oven to 400F/205C. Rub chicken breasts with oil and season with salt and pepper. Place on a baking sheet and bake for 15 minutes, flip, and bake for another 10 minutes until chicken is cooked through, no longer pink, and juices run clear. Set aside.
2. Prepare rice as per package directions. Chop or shred the chicken breast and mix with 2-3 tablespoons of BBQ sauce until the meat is well coated.
3. Drain and rinse the black beans. Cut the zucchini into small cubes (1/4-1/2"), shred the pepper jack, slice the green onions, and pit and slice the avocado.
4. To build the bowls place 1 cup cooked rice in the bottom of each bowl. Divide the chicken, beans, corn, zucchini, shredded cheese, green onions, and avocado slices equally among all four bowls. Drizzle one more tablespoon of BBQ sauce over top and serve.

Red Velvet Pancakes

Serves: 4 Calories: 650

Cooking Time: 45 minutes

Ingredients

RED VELVET PANCAKES

- 2 cups red velvet cake mix
- 3 tablespoons melted butter
- 1 egg
- 1 cup whole milk
- Nonstick spray, for cooking

CREAM CHEESE ICING

- 6 tablespoons whipped cream cheese
- 4 tablespoons confectioners' sugar
- 4 tablespoons heavy cream
- ¼ teaspoon vanilla extract

Directions

1. Make the pancakes: In a large bowl, whisk the cake mix with the butter, egg and milk to combine. Work out any lumps with the whisk to make sure the batter is smooth.
2. Heat a medium nonstick skillet over high heat. When the skillet is hot, spritz it with nonstick spray and reduce the heat to low (to prevent the pancakes from becoming too dark).
3. Working in batches, ladle the batter into the skillet and cook until bubbles begin to rise from the center of the pancakes, 2 to 3 minutes. Flip the pancakes and continue cooking 1 to 2 minutes more. Remove the pancakes to a plate and cover with a towel to keep warm.
4. Make the icing: Using a whisk or hand mixer, combine the cream cheese with the sugar, cream and vanilla.
5. To serve, pile the pancakes onto plates and top generously with icing.

Onion & Arugula Frittata

Serves: 4 Calories: 305

Cooking Time: 50 minutes

Ingredients

- 1 tablespoon olive oil
- 2 medium sweet onions, thinly sliced
- Kosher salt
- Pinch of red pepper flakes
- 4 cups arugula
- 3 whole eggs
- 5 egg whites
- ⅓ cup skim milk
- ¼ cup goat cheese crumbles

Directions

1. Preheat the oven to 350F/180C. Heat the olive oil in a medium oven-safe skillet over medium heat. Add the onions, reduce the heat to low and cook the onions until they're golden brown and caramelized, 20 to 25 minutes.
2. Season the onions to taste with salt and red pepper flakes. Add the arugula and cook until wilted, 1 to 2 minutes. Raise the heat to medium high.
3. In a medium bowl, whisk the eggs, egg whites and milk to combine. Pour the mixture into the pan and let it cook for 2 to 3 minutes to set the base. Sprinkle the crumbled goat cheese on top of the egg mixture.
4. Transfer the pan to the oven and bake until the frittata is set, 15 to 20 minutes. Let cool for 5 minutes before serving. The frittata can be served warm, at room temperature or chilled.

Sweet Crepes with Caramelized Pears

Serves: 4 Calories: 305

Cooking Time: 40 minutes

Ingredients

CREPES

- 1 cup milk
- ¼ cup water
- 2 eggs
- 4 tablespoons melted butter, plus more for the pan
- ¾ teaspoon pure vanilla extract
- 1 cup all-purpose flour
- Pinch of cinnamon

FILLING AND FINISHING

- 1½ cups mascarpone cheese
- ¼ cup heavy cream
- ½ cup confectioners' sugar, plus more for garnish
- 1 tablespoon butter
- 2 pears-halved, cored and thinly sliced
- 3 tablespoons brown sugar
- Pinch of cinnamon
- 1-pint blackberries
- Honey, for garnish

Directions

1. **MAKE THE CREPES:** In a large bowl, whisk the milk with the water, eggs, butter and vanilla extract to combine. Add the flour and cinnamon, and mix to combine. If the mixture looks lumpy, strain it to remove the lumps. (If making ahead, the batter can now be stored, refrigerated, for up to two days.)

2. **COOK THE CREPES:** Brush a medium nonstick skillet or crepe pan with melted butter (about 1 teaspoon) and heat over medium-high heat. When the pan is hot, use a small ladle or ½-cup measuring cup to pour batter into the pan; pour in a circular motion to cover the whole base of the pan. (You can also lift the pan off the burner and swirl the batter around the base to spread it evenly.)

3. Cook the crepe until the edge looks lacy and golden, 2 to 3 minutes. Use a rubber spatula to loosen the crepe around the edge, then vigorously shake the pan back and forth to loosen the entire crepe from the base of the pan.

4. Use the spatula to carefully flip the crepe and cook for an additional 30 seconds to 1 minute on the other side, or until lightly golden. Transfer the crepe to a plate and top with a piece of parchment or waxed paper. Repeat steps 2 to 4 until all the batter has been used.

5. **MAKE THE FILLING:** In a small bowl, whisk the mascarpone with the cream and confectioners' sugar to combine. Set aside.

6. In a large sauté pan, heat the butter over medium heat. Add the pear slices, brown sugar and cinnamon; cook, tossing occasionally, until the pears are golden and soft, 4 to 5 minutes.

7. **FILL THE CREPES:** To serve, place 2 tablespoons mascarpone cream, 3 tablespoons pear mixture and a few fresh blackberries in the center of each crepe. Then fold the crepe into quarters and set on a plate. Finish with a sprinkle of confectioners' sugar and/or a drizzle of honey.

2. Immunity Boosting Smoothies

If you want to be Ok – drink Smoothies Every Day!

Smoothies – the Best part of your Breakfast!

Lush, colorful, creamy, and chunky... Welcome to the world of glorious smoothies!

Giving you the benefit of not just the juice but also the pulp (or peel) alongside added ingredients, smoothies are a great option for you to make a part of your daily life. Vitamins, minerals, acids, and good fats all form a part of many fruits and vegetables, and these remain in their native, wholesome form when you run that blender. Better than cooked food sources of nutrients, an organic smoothie will deliver a daily dose of unadulterated nutrition that can help achieve a higher state of wellbeing for you and your family.

The immunity boosting smoothie recipes created out of the choicest seasonal and everyday ingredients will fight everything from flu to allergies. And combined with a nutritious diet, these will act as a deterrent to many infectious diseases. Especially ideal for bugs caught during season changes, fortify yourself and everyone around with these, well in time, to stay healthy and disease free.

Inspiration for that delicious, perfectly blended smoothie need not remain just limited to everyday ingredients. Experimentation remains key, and with each mix, you will discover just how limitless the smoothie world is!

Flu-Fighter Blackberry Smoothie

This power-packed immunity-boosting smoothie, filled with the goodness of herbs and honey is especially ideal for consumption during seasonal weather change. The basil boosts your tolerance, the blackberries provide a high-dose of antioxidants, and the mint keeps your digestive system running efficiently.

Serves: 1   Calories: 133

Preparation Time: 5 minutes

Ingredients

• Fresh blackberries	1 cup
• Greek yoghurt	½ cup
• Honey	1 tablespoon
• Apple juice	½ cup
• Basil	4 to 5 leaves
• Mint	4 to 5 leaves
• Extra mint	For garnish

Method

1. Blend the yoghurt and apple juice together till runny and consistent.
2. Add the cup of blackberries, basil and mint leaves, and run your blender for a few minutes till the mixture is properly smooth.
3. Add the spoon of honey at last and blend till ready.
4. Serve in a tall glass topped with a sprig of fresh mint on top.

Raspberry Chia Healer Smoothie

Magical chia seeds have many benefits. From your skin, to your heart, to your digestive system, healing chia will provide many immune-boosting qualities. The unique fatty acids in coconut milk provide anti-bacterial, anti-fungal, and anti-viral properties, while the berries aid in everything ranging from allergies to low-blood sugar.

Serves: 1   Calories: 360

Preparation Time: 7 minutes

Ingredients

• Fresh raspberries	A handful
• Coconut milk	¼ cup
• Chia seeds	2 tablespoons
• Skim milk	½ cup
• Elderberry extract	1 teaspoon

Method

1. Soak the chia seeds overnight to be used in the morning for making this recipe.

2. In a blender, mix the coconut milk, milk, and elderberry extract together and blend till smooth and creamy. Pour the smoothie base into a serving glass

3. Drain the water from the chia seeds, and stir into the smoothie base gently mixing it all up till it is consistent.

4. Before serving, top up the glass with the fresh raspberries.

Spinach Booster Smoothie

Greens such as spinach, kale, and celery are packed with vitamin C that will help fight not just infections but other immune compromising factors. Ginger is one of the best natural guards against flu, and will drain toxins from your body. Add to this, a dash of Himalayan pink salt for a booster dose of minerals and taste!

Serves: 1   Calories: 70

Preparation Time: 5 minutes

Ingredients

• Baby spinach	1 cup
• Kale	½ cup
• Celery	½ cup
• Ginger paste	½ teaspoon
• Vegetable stock	1 cup
• Himalayan pink salt	A pinch
• Almonds	5

Method

1. Blend the spinach, celery, and kale into a smooth paste.

2. To this mixture, add the vegetable stock and create a runny consistency.

3. Add the ginger paste and almonds, blending for a while more till the smoothie is fragrant and there are no chewable bits.

4. Pour into serving glass and sprinkle with the Himalayan pink salt.

The Magic of Red Smoothie

There's a reason why you are told to consume your reds. Cranberries protect the good bacteria in your gut and help with an array of infections. Plums will promote cardiovascular health. Pomegranates will kill disease-causing bacteria in your stomach. Together, they are an immune-boosting force to be reckoned with.

Serves: 1   Calories: 173

Preparation Time: 5 minutes

Ingredients

• Pitted cranberries	1 cup
• Pitted plums	½ cup
• Pomegranate	½ cup
• Lime juice	2 tablespoons
• Brown sugar	1 teaspoon
• Extra cranberries	A few chunks

Method

1. In a blender, put together the pitted cranberries and plums and shred until a paste-like consistency is reached.

2. Add the pomegranate and the lime juice to this mixture and run the blender for a while more, so that the mixture is runny.

3. Finally add the brown sugar and serve in a glass along with a few chunks of cranberries added to the smoothie.

Peach Power Smoothie

Juicy peaches, loaded with vitamin A will help with your immune function, while bananas are loaded with minerals like zinc and selenium. Walnuts are a great source of good fatty acids, and the oatmeal will provide a rich creamy base for your smoothie. A hearty, filling version of this recipe is great for a good start to your day.

Serves: 1   Calories: 400

Preparation Time: 10 minutes

Ingredients

- Pitted and skinned peaches   1 cup
- Banana   1, medium sized
- Skim milk   1 cup
- Walnuts   A handful
- Cooked oatmeal   2 tablespoons

Method

1. Begin by blending the peach and milk together.
2. Add the banana to this mixture, and blend until there are no lumps of fruit left behind in the smoothie.
3. Add the walnuts and oatmeal and run the blender for 30 seconds.
4. Serve in a tall glass, ideally for breakfast.

3. Meat

Spinach Steak Pinwheels

Serves: 4   Calories: 369

Preparation Time: 15 minutes

Ingredients

- 1½ pounds beef top sirloin steak
- 8 bacon strips, cooked and drained
- 1 package (10 ounces) frozen and chopped spinach, thawed and squeezed dry
- ¼ cup grated Parmesan cheese
- ⅛ Teaspoon cayenne pepper and salt

Method

1. Make diagonal cuts in steak at 1-inch intervals to within ½ inch of bottom of meat. Repeat cuts in opposite direction. Pound to ½-inch thickness. Place bacon down the center of the meat.
2. In a large bowl, combine the spinach, Parmesan cheese, salt, and cayenne; spoon over bacon.
3. Roll up and secure with toothpicks. Cut into six slices.
4. Grill, uncovered, over medium heat for 6 minutes on each side or until meat reaches desired doneness (for medium-rare, a meat thermometer should read 145F/65C; medium, 160F/70C; well-done, 170F/75C).
5. Discard toothpicks and serve.

Roast Beef and Gravy

Serves: 4   Calories: 250

Preparation Time: 35 minutes

Ingredients

- 1 (3 to 4-pound) bone-in rib-eye roast
- Kosher salt and freshly ground black pepper

For the gravy:

- 1 large shallot, finely chopped
- ½ bottle drinking red wine, such as Malbec
- 5 cups beef stock

Method

1. Using a heavy hand, season rib-eye roast with salt and pepper on all sides. Heat olive oil in a large Dutch oven or a roasting pan.
2. Place beef in hot pan and sear until deep golden brown on all sides.
3. Transfer the pan to the oven and roast for about 15 minutes per pound for medium-rare, making an approximate hour of cooking time.
4. Remove the pan from oven and transfer the beef to a cutting board. Allow meat to rest for at least 15 minutes, tented with foil, before carving.
5. To make the gravy: Pour off excess fat from the Dutch oven and place the pan on the stovetop over medium heat. Add shallots and cook until soft and brown, about 4 to 6 minutes.
6. Deglaze the pot with ½ cup of the wine, scraping up browned bits from the bottom. Add remaining wine, bring to a boil, and reduce by half.
7. Add stock and simmer until reduced again by about half. Pass the gravy through a fine mesh sieve and return to the pan.

8. Bring back to a boil, then lower the heat and simmer until desired gravy consistency is reached. Taste for seasoning and adjust, if necessary. Carve beef against the grain, into thin slices, and serve with gravy.

Beef and Vegetable Stir Fry

Serves: 4 Calories: 234

Preparation Time: 20 minutes

Ingredients

- 1 tablespoon olive oil
- 1 (16-ounce) package frozen mixed vegetables
- 1 cup stir fry sauce with water
- 2 teaspoons cornstarch
- 2 cups cubed cooked roast beef

Method

1. Heat the olive oil in a heavy skillet. When the oil is hot, add the frozen vegetables and 1 tablespoon of water, then stir.
2. Cover the pan and cook vegetables over medium heat for 3 minutes.
3. Meanwhile, combine the stir fry sauce and cornstarch in a small bowl. Pour into the skillet with the vegetables and stir.
4. Then add the cooked beef and stir again. Replace the cover and cook the beef and vegetables for 5 to 8 minutes over low heat, stirring occasionally, until the beef if hot and the vegetables tender yet still crisp.

Moist & Tender Chicken Breasts

Serves: 4   Calories: 220

Preparation Time: 30 minutes

Ingredients

- 1 to 4 boneless, skinless chicken breasts, of similar size
- Pinch of salt
- Freshly ground black pepper
- 1 tablespoon olive oil
- Unsalted butter

Method

1. Flatten the chicken breasts: Pound the chicken breasts to an even thickness with the bottom of a wide jar or glass. You can also (carefully!) use the handle of a heavy chef's knife.
2. Season the chicken breasts: Lightly salt and pepper the chicken breasts.
3. Prepare the pan: Heat the fry pan over medium-high heat. When it is quite hot, add the olive oil (or butter, if using). Swirl the pan so it is lightly covered with the olive oil.
4. Cook the chicken breasts for 1 minute without moving: Turn the heat to medium. Add the chicken breasts. Cook for just about 1 minute to help them get a little golden on one side (you are not actually searing or browning them).
5. Flip the chicken breasts: Then flip each chicken breast over.
6. Turn the heat down to low: Turn the heat to low.
7. Cover the pan and cook on low for 10 minutes. Cover with a tight-fitting lid. Set a timer for 10 minutes, and walk away. Do not lift the lid; do not peek.

8. Turn off the heat and let sit for an additional 10 minutes: After 10 minutes have elapsed, turn off the heat. (If you have an electric stove, remove the pan from the heat.) Reset the timer for 10 minutes and leave the chicken breasts in the pan. Again, do not lift the lid; do not peek.

9. Remove lid and take temperature: After the 10 minutes are up, take the lid off, and your chicken is done. Make sure there is no pink in the middle of the chicken breasts. If you want to be absolutely sure it is cooked, you can use an instant-read thermometer to check (the chicken should be at least 165F/75C). Slice and eat. Store any leftovers in a covered container in the refrigerator.

Lemon Garlic Chicken

Serves: 4 Calories: 190

Preparation Time: 45 minutes

Ingredients

- 1 package of chicken thighs & drumsticks (4 thighs & 4 drumsticks)
- 3 lemons
- 15 cloves of garlic, peeled
- Salt & pepper to taste
- 2 tablespoons fresh thyme leaves

Method

1. In a bowl, add the chicken pieces. Slice the lemons in half and juice them. Add the juice and the lemon rinds to the bowl, along with the garlic, salt, pepper, and thyme.
2. Mix well with your hands, then dump this all in a large baking dish.
3. Put the dish in the oven and bake the chicken for 30 to 40 minutes, basting every 10 minutes.
4. When the skin gets crispy and the meat is cooked through, it is done.

Homemade Chicken Nuggets

Serves: 4   Calories: approx. 285

Preparation Time: 40 minutes

Ingredients

- 2-3 chicken breast fillets (about 600g)
- ½ cup plain flour
- 2 eggs
- 4 slices day old bread
- 1/3 cup cornflake crumbs
- 1/3 cup freshly grated parmesan cheese
- ½ cup mayonnaise
- 2 tbsp sweet chili sauce

Method

1. Tear bread into pieces and whiz in a food processor to get fine breadcrumbs.
2. Slice chicken breasts into bite-sized pieces.
3. Put the flour on a large square of baking paper.
4. Whisk eggs in a small bowl.
5. Mix breadcrumbs, cornflake crumbs and parmesan cheese in a bowl.
6. Coat the chicken pieces in flour, dust off, dip in egg wash and then coat in crumb mix. You may need to press the crumbs on. Place the coated chicken pieces onto a baking tray lined with baking paper. Refrigerate for 30 minutes.
7. Preheat oven to 360F / 180C and bake the chicken for 10 minutes or until cooked through.
8. To make the dipping sauce, combine mayonnaise and sweet chili sauce in a small bowl.
9. Serve nuggets with dipping sauce.

Chicken and Antipasto Rice

Serves: 3   Calories: approx. 330

Preparation Time: 30 minutes

Ingredients

- 2 chicken breast fillets
- 1 x 225 g jar antipasto vegetables in oil
- 3 cups cooked brown rice

Method

1. Slice chicken fillets horizontally into thin scallops.
2. Place in a bowl and pour over some of the oil from the antipasto, ensuring it is well coated.
3. Heat a non-stick frypan over medium heat.
4. Fry chicken for 1-2 minutes on each side until just cooked through. Set aside and keep warm.
5. Remove vegetables from oil and dice.
6. Pour one tablespoon of remaining oil into the frypan and add vegetables and cooked rice.
7. Stir to combine and warm through.
8. Distribute rice between serving bowls and top with chicken.

4. Salads

Making salad a regular part of your diet has plenty of upsides – it's a quick, easy way to get more vegetables into your diet, a way to sample new recipes from around the world and expand your palate – and although they're generally surprisingly easy to make, there are few things that look more impressive on the dinner table than a big, colorful mixed salad! Not to mention, of course, the fact that they're delicious, and so varied that there's really something for everyone, from health-conscious vegans to picky children who won't usually even look at a vegetable. With all these benefits, salad really is a must-have dish to add to your cooking repertoire.

One of the most important aspects of any salad, of course, is the ingredients – with many salads featuring uncooked or cold food, it's extra important for everything to be fresh, high-quality and delicious. Luckily, choosing the best ingredients at the store is easy once you know what you're doing – look for the freshest veg, unpackaged where possible so you can check it thoroughly. Make sure the vegetables and fruit you pick aren't bruised, too soft, or starting to get dull, wrinkly skin. For avocados, it's usually better to buy slightly under-ripe fruit and let it ripen at home for a day or two, so you can grab it and use it when it's at its best – there should be a little give when you squeeze it, but not so much that it feels soft and mushy.

Another great thing about salads is that, with a few exceptions, they're very easy to cook and prepare! The most important thing you'll need is a good, sharp knife – lots of chopping, dicing and slicing is involved and a good quality knife will make it much easier and the results will look far better. Many salads can be served immediately, especially those with fresh salad leaves, but a lot will benefit from having time to sit and refrigerate to allow the flavors to mingle.

Finally, a wonderful benefit of salads is how customizable they are!

Twisty Egg Salad

You will love the taste of this pasta along with the vegetables and eggs ingredients.

Serves: 2   Calories: 170

Preparation Time: 15 minutes

Ingredients

- Pasta twists–2 cups
- Boiled eggs–2
- Celery sticks–2
- Red capsicum(sliced) –1
- Green onions(chopped) –2
- Parsley leaves2 cups
- Egg mayonnaise–2 tbsp.
- Wholegrain mustard–2 tbsp.
- Lemon juice–2 tbsp.

Method

1. Boil the pasta twists for 10 minutes and rinse them when ready.
2. Add boiled eggs, celery sticks, red capsicum and green onion into the bowl.
3. Add oil into the pan and cook the mixture.
4. When done, add parsley, mayonnaise, mustard and lemon juice.
5. Mix well.
6. Mix both pasta and mixture into a large bowl.
7. When ready, serve.

Ultimate Cobb Salad with Poppy Seed Dressing

Packed with a variety of delicious ingredients, this filling salad makes a great summer lunch.

Serves: 4   Calories: 220

Preparation Time: 20 minutes

Ingredients:
Dressing
- ⅓ cup full-fat mayo
- ¼ cup whole milk
- 2 tbsp. sugar
- 1 tbsp. apple cider vinegar
- 1 tbsp. poppy seeds

Salad
- 4 rashers unsmoked bacon (diced)
- 6 cups lettuce of choice
- 2 hardboiled eggs (chopped)
- 1 red apple (chopped)
- 1 pear (chopped)
- ½ cup pecans (chopped)
- ⅓ cup dried pecans
- ⅓ cup goat cheese (crumbled)

Method

1. Combine all dressing ingredients in a bowl, stir well and set aside.
2. Sauté the bacon pieces in a skillet over med-high heat, until crispy.
3. Transfer to a plate and pat away any excess grease with kitchen paper. Set aside.
4. Into the base of a large salad bowl, make a bed of lettuce.
5. Arrange the remaining ingredients in rows on top of the lettuce and then drizzle over the poppy seed dressing.

Egg Salad

Losing weight is not easy; this recipe will help your stomach filled along with providing essential nutrients.

Serves: 2   Calories: 170

Preparation Time: 10 minutes

Ingredients

- Eggs–2
- Lettuce–2 cups
- Cucumber–1
- Micro cress–1 cup
- Greek yogurt–1 cup
- Curry powder–2 tbsp.
- Oil–2 tbsp.
- Cayenne pepper 2 tbsp.
- Nigella seeds–1 tsp.

Method

1. Add eggs into the bowl.
2. Mix lettuce, cucumber, micro cress, cayenne pepper and nigella seeds.
3. Add oil and yogurt.
4. Mix well.
5. Chill in fridge for 10 minutes.
6. When ready, serve!

Wholegrain Salad with Shallot Yoghurt Dressing

This sophisticated salad is packed with wholegrain goodness.

Serves: 4 Calories: 180

Preparation Time: 1 hour 15 minutes

Ingredients

- ½ cup rye berries
- 1 shallot (chopped)
- ¾ cup full-fat Greek yogurt
- 2 tbsp. fresh mint (chopped)
- 1 tbsp. freshly squeezed lemon juice
- Sea salt and black pepper (to taste)
- 6 cups salad greens
- 4 eggs soft boiled (halved)

Method

1. Bring a large pot of salted water to a boil. Toss in the rye berries and cook for just over an hour, or until tender. Drain away the water and allow to cool.
2. In a small bowl, combine the shallots, Greek yogurt, chopped mint and half of the lemon juice.
3. Stir well and season with sea salt and black pepper.
4. Add the salad greens and cooled rye berries to a large serving bowl.
5. Pour over the remaining lemon juice and toss well.
6. Arrange the halved soft-boiled eggs on top and drizzle over the yogurt dressing.
7. Serve!

Black Rice and Spinach Salad *(TOP)*

Serves: 4   Calories: 210

Preparation Time: 15 minutes

Ingredients

- 3 cups cooked black rice forbidden
- 2 cups baby spinach
- 1 cup sliced strawberries
- 1 cup blueberries
- 1/2 -1 cup pistachios
- 50-100 grams feta

Dressing:

- 1/2 cup olive oil
- 1/4 cup vinegar
- 2 cloves garlic chopped
- 1/4 cup fresh orange juice
- Salt and pepper to taste

Method

1. Mix all ingredients together in a large bowl.
2. Mix all dressing ingredients in a jar and shake.
3. Dress salad and mix well.
4. Feel free to add feta.
5. Serve, enjoy!

Roasted Vegetable Couscous Salad

Serves: 4   Calories: approx. 500

Preparation Time: 30 mins - 2 hours

Ingredients

- 1 red bell pepper
- 1 yellow bell pepper
- 1 onion
- 1 zucchini
- 3 garlic cloves
- 2 tbsp. olive oil
- 1 cup couscous
- pinch of salt
- pinch of black pepper
- 1 tbsp. lemon juice

Method

1. Pre-heat the oven to 200C / 400F.
2. Slice the onions, bell peppers and zucchini.
3. Mix the veg and place them all in a baking tray along with the garlic cloves.
4. Roast them for 20 minutes, check on them and stir, then put them back in for another 20 minutes.
5. While they're heating up, cook the couscous: place it in a large bowl or pan, pour 1 cup of boiling water over it, cover it, and allow it to steam for five minutes.
6. Add the roasted vegetables to the couscous and season with the salt, pepper and lemon juice.
7. Refrigerate for a few hours or serve immediately for a warm salad.

5. Sandwiches

Spinach, Hummus, and Bell Pepper Wraps

Serves: 4 Calories: 258

Preparation Time: 10 minutes

Ingredients

- 2 (1.9-oz.) whole-grain flatbreads (such as Flatout Light)
- 1/2 cup roasted garlic hummus
- 1 small red bell pepper, thinly sliced
- 1 cup firmly packed baby spinach
- 1 ounce crumbled tomato-and-basil feta cheese (about 1/4 cup)

Method

1. Spread each flatbread with 1/4 cup hummus, leaving a 1/2-inch border around the edge.
2. Divide the bell pepper evenly between the flatbreads; top each with 1/2 cup spinach and 2 tablespoons cheese.
3. Starting from one short side, roll up the wraps.
4. Cut each wrap in half, and secure with wooden picks.

Waffle Iron Turkey Melt Panini

Serves: 4 Calories: 369

Preparation Time: 10 minutes

Ingredients

- 4 center-cut bacon slices
- 3 tablespoons canola mayonnaise
- 1 teaspoon Dijon mustard & cheese
- 8 (1-ounce) slices whole-grain or whole-wheat bread
- 8 ounces unsalted sliced deli turkey & apple

Method

1. Preheat a waffle iron with 4 compartments to HIGH.
2. Place a paper towel on a microwave-safe plate.
3. Arrange bacon on paper towel; cover with an additional paper towel.
4. Microwave bacon at HIGH for 4 minutes or until done.
5. Combine mayonnaise and mustard in a small bowl.
6. Spread about 1 1/4 teaspoons mayonnaise mixture over each bread slice. Divide bacon, turkey, apple slices, and cheese evenly among 4 bread slices; top with remaining bread slices, spread side down.
7. Lightly coat both sides of sandwiches with cooking spray.
8. Place 1 sandwich in each compartment of waffle iron; close waffle iron firmly on sandwiches.
9. Place a heavy skillet on top of waffle iron to help flatten sandwiches evenly.
10. Cook 3 to 4 minutes or until golden brown and cheese melts.

Prosciutto, Fontina, and Fig Panini

Serves: 4 Calories: 345

Preparation Time: 5 minutes

Ingredients

- 8 (0.9-ounce) slices crusty Chicago-style Italian bread
- 4 ounces very thinly sliced prosciutto
- 1 1/4 cups (4 ounces) shredded fontina cheese
- 1/2 cup baby arugula leaves
- 1/4 cup fig preserves

Method

1. Preheat panini grill.
2. Top each of 4 bread slices evenly with prosciutto, fontina cheese, and arugula.
3. Spread 1 tablespoon fig preserves evenly over 1 side of each of remaining 4 bread slices; top sandwiches with remaining bread slices.
4. Coat outsides of sandwiches with cooking spray.
5. Place sandwiches on panini grill; cook 3 to 4 minutes or until golden and cheese is melted.
6. Cut panini in half before serving, if desired.

Hummus-Zucchini English Muffin

Serves: 4   Calories: 229

Preparation Time: 5 minutes

Ingredients

- 2 tablespoons hummus
- 1 toasted whole-grain English muffin, split
- 2 tablespoons shaved carrot
- 2 tablespoons shaved zucchini
- 2 teaspoons roasted salted sunflower seeds

Method

1. Spread hummus on cut sides of English muffin halves.
2. Top with carrot, zucchini, and sunflower seeds.

Grilled Ham, Muenster, and Spinach Sandwiches

Serves: 4 Calories: 315

Preparation Time: 7 minutes

Ingredients

- 8 (3/4-ounce) slices crusty Chicago-style Italian bread (about 1/2 inch thick), toasted
- 8 ounces thinly sliced lower-sodium deli ham
- 4 (1-ounce) slices reduced-sodium Muenster cheese
- 2 cups fresh baby spinach
- 1/4 cup mild chowchow

Method

1. Layer each of 4 bread slices with 2 ounces ham, 1 slice Muenster cheese, 1/2 cup baby spinach, 1 tablespoon chowchow, and 1 bread slice.
2. Heat a large nonstick skillet over medium-high heat.
3. Coat sandwiches with cooking spray; add to pan.
4. Cook 2 minutes on each side or until browned and cheese melts.
5. Cut sandwiches in half, if desired.
6. Serve immediately.

6. Soups and Broth

Beefy Corn and Black Bean Chili

Serves: 6   Calories: 193

Preparation Time: 20 minutes

Ingredients

- 1 pound ground round
- 2 teaspoons salt-free chili powder blend
- 1 (14-ounce) package frozen seasoned corn and black beans
- 1 (14-ounce) can fat-free, less-sodium beef broth
- 1 (15-ounce) can seasoned tomato sauce for chili

Method

1. Combine beef and chili powder blend in a large Dutch oven. Cook 6 minutes over medium-high heat or until beef is browned, stirring to crumble. Drain and return to pan.
2. Stir in frozen corn mixture, broth, and tomato sauce; bring to a boil. Cover, reduce heat, and simmer 10 minutes.
3. Uncover and simmer 5 minutes, stirring occasionally.
4. Ladle chili into bowls.
5. Top each serving with sour cream and onions, if desired.

Posole

Serves: 6   Calories: 233

Preparation Time: 20 minutes

Ingredients

- 1 (1-pound) pork tenderloin, trimmed and cut into bite-sized pieces
- 2 teaspoons salt-free Southwest chipotle seasoning blend
- 1 (15.5-ounce) can white hominy, undrained
- 1 (14.5-ounce) can Mexican-style stewed tomatoes with jalapeno peppers and spices, undrained
- 1/4 cup chopped fresh cilantro

Method

1. Heat a large saucepan over medium-high heat. Coat pan with cooking spray.
2. Sprinkle pork evenly with chipotle seasoning blend; coat evenly with cooking spray.
3. Add pork to pan; cook 4 minutes or until browned. Stir in hominy, tomatoes, and 1 cup water.
4. Bring to a boil; cover, reduce heat, and simmer 20 minutes or until pork is tender. Stir in cilantro.

Spicy Poblano and Corn Soup

Serves: 6   Calories: 239

Preparation Time: 10 minutes

Ingredients

- 1 (16-ounce) package frozen baby gold and white corn, thawed and divided
- 2 cups fat-free milk, divided
- 4 poblano chiles, seeded and chopped (about 1 pound)
- 1 cup refrigerated prechopped onion
- 1/2 cup (2 ounces) reduced-fat shredded sharp cheddar cheese

Method

1. Place 1 cup corn and 1 1/2 cups milk in a Dutch oven. Bring mixture to a boil over medium heat.
2. Combine chopped chile, onion, and 1 tablespoon water in a microwave-safe bowl. Cover and microwave at HIGH 4 minutes.
3. Meanwhile, place 2 cups corn and 1/2 cup milk in a blender; process until smooth.
4. Add pureed mixture to corn mixture in pan. Stir in chile mixture and salt, and cook 6 minutes over medium heat.
5. Ladle soup into bowls, and top each serving with 2 tablespoons cheddar cheese.

Southwestern Chicken and White Bean Soup

Serves: 4   Calories: 134

Preparation Time: 15 minutes

Ingredients

- 2 cups shredded cooked chicken breast
- 1 tablespoon 40%-less-sodium taco seasoning
- 2 (14-ounce) cans fat-free, less-sodium chicken broth
- 1 (16-ounce) can cannellini beans or other white beans, rinsed and drained
- 1/2 cup green salsa

Method

1. Combine chicken and taco seasoning; toss well to coat. Heat a large saucepan over medium-high heat. Coat pan with cooking spray.
2. Add chicken; cook for 2 minutes or until chicken is lightly browned.
3. Add broth, scraping pan to loosen browned bits.
4. Place beans in a small bowl; mash until only a few whole beans remain.
5. Add beans and salsa to pan, stirring well. Bring to a boil.
6. Reduce heat; simmer 10 minutes or until slightly thick.
7. Serve with sour cream and cilantro, if desired.

Chicken-Escarole Soup

Serves: 4   Calories: 118

Preparation Time: 10 minutes

Ingredients

- 1 (14 1/2-ounce) can Italian-style stewed tomatoes, undrained and chopped
- 1 (14-ounce) can fat-free, less-sodium chicken broth
- 1 cup chopped cooked chicken breast
- 2 cups coarsely chopped escarole (about 1 small head)
- 2 teaspoons extra-virgin olive oil

Method

1. Combine tomatoes and broth in a large saucepan.
2. Cover and bring to a boil over high heat.
3. Reduce heat to low; simmer 5 minutes.
4. Add chicken, escarole, and oil; cook 5 minutes.

Simple Pumpkin Soup

Serves: 8   Calories: approx. 180

Cook time: 30 minutes

Ingredients

- 1 butternut pumpkin, peeled de-seeded and cubed
- 1 large potato, peeled and cubed
- 1 large carrot, peeled and roughly chopped
- 1 onion, diced
- 2 tbsp. olive oil
- 4 tbsp. Massel chicken flavoured stock powder

Method

1. Heat oil in a pan and fry all vegetables until golden.
2. Add 2L boiling water to the pan and stir in stock powder.
3. Bring to the boil and simmer for 20 minutes until all vegetables are soft.
4. Using a stick mixer liquefy all the soup until it's nice and smooth.
5. Taste and season with salt and pepper accordingly.

7. Lunch Box

Lunch is an important meal of the midday and you get the energy to work through the afternoon and to prevent you from crashing till you get your dinner. When you are having the lunch long hours after the breakfast, you are re- energizing the body. When the blood sugar levels go down it affects the concentration on the work you are doing. A good healthy and filling lunch can bring back the sugar levels to the optimum and you will feel refreshed for next 3-4 hours.

Reasons To Have Healthy Lunch

Here are some important reasons to have a healthy home packed lunch

- Lunch provides the much needed energy during the mid-day
- Having a proper lunch avoids the chances binge eating
- Taking a lunch break from the work helps you to get refreshed and keep away the tensions of the job for a while.
- You can have healthy and low- calorie lunch and you need not have to depend on junk foods to curb the appetite.
- You will be saving lots of money when you are having a home packed lunch.
- Missing the lunch will make a person feel sleepy and lethargic

What To Consider While Preparing The Lunch Box Item?

When you are preparing the lunch box you need to consider various factors. The important things to consider while preparing the lunch box includes

- **The Age Of The Person**

You have to prepare the lunch according to the age of the person having the particular lunch.

- **The Nutrition**

It is necessary that the lunch box should contain a nutritional diet. The recipe for the lunch should include carbohydrate, proteins, vitamins and minerals necessary for the body to work normally.

- **Simple And Easy To Make**

Preparing the lunch should be an easy task. So select recipes with simple ingredients and which are easy to make. You may not get time to prepare an elaborate healthy lunch in the morning.

- **Avoid Repetition**

Preparing the same recipes again and again may create an aversion to the particular item. So try to make new lunch recipes every now and then and avoid repeating the same menu for at least a week.

- **Plan The Menu Earlier**

You can plan the menu for the lunch earlier itself. This will help to avoid unnecessary buying of groceries and avoiding the use of pre-prepared food that are rich in fat content.

Quick Salmon Burger

Serves: 1   Calories: 133

Preparation Time: 8 minutes

Ingredients

- 1 salmon patty
- 1 tablespoon lemon juice
- 2 tablespoons Djion mustard
- 1 whole-grain bun
- Lettuce and tomato, sliced

Method

1. Heat oil in a pan and cook salmon patty on both sides. Sprinkle lemon juice over the patty.
2. Spread Dijon mustard on both sides of a whole-grain bun. Assemble salmon patty, lettuce and tomato slices in bun.

Fuss-Free Frittata

Serves: 1   Calories: 230

Preparation Time: 8 minutes

Ingredients

- 4 whole eggs
- 1 cup red bell peppers, chopped
- 1 cup mushrooms, chopped
- 1 cup frozen peas

Method

1. In a small bowl, beat the eggs together. Add the mixture to a skillet pan, allowing eggs to set.
2. Scatter the bell peppers, mushrooms and peas over the mixture.
3. When eggs are cooked, use a spatula to slide frittata out of the pan and serve.

Old school lunch

Serves: 1   Calories: 160

Preparation Time: 10 minutes

Ingredients

For smoothie:

- 1/2 cup frozen strawberries
- 1 banana
- 1 cup nonfat milk

For sandwich:

- 1 slice whole-grain bread
- 4 slices smoked turkey breast
- Lettuce and tomato

Method

1. To make the smoothie, combine frozen strawberries, banana and milk together in a blender.
2. To make the sandwich, slice bread in half, spread Dijon mustard on each side, then layer turkey breast, lettuce and tomato between the halves.
3. Serve with fruit of choice, like grapes, blueberries and a banana.

Lemon Pepper Shrimp Scampi

Serves: 4   Calories: 403

Preparation Time: 15 minutes

Ingredients

- 1 cup uncooked orzo
- 2 tablespoons chopped fresh parsley
- 1/2 teaspoon salt, divided
- 7 teaspoons unsalted butter, divided
- 1 1/2 pounds peeled and deveined jumbo shrimp
- 2 teaspoons minced fresh garlic
- 2 tablespoons fresh lemon juice
- 1/4 teaspoon freshly ground black pepper

Method

1. Cook orzo according to package directions, omitting salt and fat. Drain. Place orzo in a medium bowl. Stir in parsley and 1/4 teaspoon salt; cover and keep warm.
2. While orzo cooks, melt 1 tablespoon butter in a large nonstick skillet over medium-high heat. Sprinkle shrimp with remaining 1/4 teaspoon salt.
3. Add half of shrimp to pan; cook 2 minutes or until almost done. Transfer shrimp to a plate. Melt 1 teaspoon butter in pan. Add remaining shrimp to pan; cook 2 minutes or until almost done. Transfer to a plate.
4. Melt remaining 1 tablespoon butter in pan. Add garlic to pan; cook 30 seconds, stirring constantly. Stir in shrimp, juice, and pepper; cook 1 minute or until shrimp are done.

Chicken Puttanesca

Serves: 4   Calories: 241

Preparation Time: 20 minutes

Ingredients

- 1 1/2 tablespoons olive oil, divided
- 4 (4-ounce) skinless, boneless chicken breast cutlets
- 1/4 cup minced fresh onion
- 3 garlic cloves, minced
- 2 cups chopped tomato
- 1/4 cup sliced green olives
- 1 tablespoon chopped fresh oregano
- 1 1/2 teaspoons capers, chopped
- 1/2 teaspoon crushed red pepper
- 1/4 teaspoon salt
- 1 canned anchovy fillet, chopped

Method

1. Heat a large nonstick skillet over medium-high heat. Add 1 tablespoon oil to pan; swirl to coat.
2. Add chicken to pan; cook 5 minutes or until done, turning once. Remove chicken from pan; keep warm.
3. Add remaining 1 1/2 teaspoons oil, onion, and garlic; sauté 1 minute.
4. Add tomato and remaining ingredients.
5. Bring to a simmer, and cook for 9 minutes or until sauce is slightly thickened, stirring occasionally.
6. Serve chicken with the tomato mixture.

Tamagoyaki - Japanese Rolled Omelet

Serves: 4   Calories: 178

Preparation Time: 5 minutes

Ingredients

- 4 eggs, beaten
- 3 tablespoons dashi soup stock
- 1 1/2 to 2 tablespoons sugar

Method

1. Beat eggs in a bowl.
2. Add dashi soup and sugar in the egg and mix well.
3. Heat a tamagoyaki pan on medium heat. Oil the pan.
4. Pour a scoop of egg mixture in the pan and spread over the surface.
5. Cook it until half done and roll the egg toward the bottom side.
6. Move the rolled egg to the top side.
7. Oil the empty part of the pan and pour another scoop of egg mixture in the space and under the rolled egg.
8. Cook it until half done and roll the egg again so that the omelet becomes thicker.
9. Cook the omelet until done.
10. If you are using a regular frying pan, shape tamagoyaki on bamboo mat.
11. Cut tamagoyaki into 1-inch thick pieces.

Teriyaki Chicken

Serves: 4   Calories: 140

Preparation Time: 30 minutes

Ingredients

- 3/4 pound boneless chicken thighs (may be substituted with chicken breasts or tenderloin)
- 2 tablespoons sake
- 4 tablespoon soy sauce
- 4 tablespoons mirin (sweet sake)
- 2 tablespoons sugar
- Pinch of grated ginger (add more to taste)
- 1 to 2 teaspoons olive oil for cooking chicken (may be substituted with canola or other oil)

Method

1. Poke chicken using a fork to help absorb the flavors of the teriyaki sauce during cooking.
2. Make the teriyaki sauce. In a large bowl, combine sake, soy sauce, mirin, sugar, and ginger and mix well.
3. Add chicken to the bowl and marinate the chicken in the teriyaki sauce for 15 minutes in the refrigerator.
4. In a large skillet, heat olive oil over medium-high heat. Place the chicken skin side down into the skillet, cooking the skin of the chicken first, until the skin is browned. Next, flip the chicken over to cook the other side, but reduce the heat to low.
5. Next, pour the teriyaki sauce that was used to marinate the chicken into the skillet. Cover the skillet with a lid and steam cook the chicken on low heat

until done, and the internal temperature of the chicken reaches 165F/75C and juices run clear.

6. Remove the lid and simmer until the sauce thickens slightly. There is no need to add potato starch or corn starch to thicken the sauce. Remove the pan from the heat.

7. Slice the chicken and serve on a plate. Pour the remaining thickened teriyaki sauce over the chicken.

8. Optional: If you like, garnish the teriyaki chicken with additional grated ginger.

Kinpira Gobo

Serves: 4   Calories: 100

Preparation Time: 15 minutes

Ingredients

- 1/2 lb gobo
- 1/4 lb carrot, peeled and cut into short and thin strips
- 1 1/2 Tbsp mirin
- 1 Tbsp sugar
- 1/2 Tbsp sake
- 1 Tbsp soy sauce
- 1 tsp sesame seeds
- 2 tsps vegetable oil

Method

1. Peel the gobo's skin with a peeler. Then diagonally slice thin strips so that each piece is about 2 inch length. Then collect some of the slices and cut into thin matchbox strips.
2. Soak the gobo strips in water for a while and drain well. You can add a drop of vinegar to the water, if desired. Change the water several times until it is clean. Leave the gobo in the water until you are ready to cook.
3. Cut the carrots into matchbox strips.
4. Heat vegetable oil in a frying pan, and fry gobo for a couple minutes.
5. Add carrot strips in the pan and stir-fry them.
6. Add sake, mirin, and sugar and stir-fry until the liquid is gone.
7. Season with soy sauce and stir-fry well.
8. Turn off the heat.
9. Sprinkle sesame seeds.

Pasta Salad

Serves: 4   Calories: 450

Preparation Time: 10 minutes

Ingredients

- 8 ounces whole-grain fusilli pasta
- 3 tablespoons extra-virgin olive oil
- 1 tablespoon red wine vinegar
- 1 teaspoon dried oregano
- 1 teaspoon dried basil
- 1 small clove garlic, minced (about 1 teaspoon)
- 1/2 teaspoon salt
- 1/4 teaspoon freshly ground black pepper
- 1 medium yellow bell pepper, diced
- 1/2 pint grape tomatoes, quartered
- 1 cup cooked, chilled, coarsely chopped broccoli
- 6 ounces fresh, part-skim mozzarella cheese, cut into 1/4-to-1/2-inch dice

Method

1. Cook the pasta al dente according to the directions on the package.
2. Drain, then transfer it to a large bowl, toss with 1 teaspoon of the oil and allow it to cool completely.
3. Whisk together in a small bowl the remaining 2 tablespoons plus 2 teaspoons of olive oil, the vinegar, oregano, basil, garlic, salt and black pepper to form a dressing.
4. Add the bell pepper, tomatoes, broccoli, mozzarella and dressing to the pasta, and toss to combine.

Chopped Kale, Farro, and Chickpea Salad

Serves: 4   Calories: 294

Preparation Time: 30 minutes

Ingredients

- 1/2 cup farro
- 1/4 teaspoon salt, plus more as needed
- 1 bunch (about 10 ounces) Tuscan, dino, or lacinato kale
- 1 tablespoon extra-virgin olive oil
- 1 teaspoon red miso paste
- 2 teaspoons lemon juice (about 1/2 lemon)
- 1 (15.5-ounce) can chickpeas, drained and rinsed

Method

1. Bring 2 cups of water to a boil in a 2-quart saucepan over medium-high heat. Stir in 1/4 teaspoon salt and the farro.
2. Reduce the heat to low and simmer uncovered for 25 to 30 minutes, until the farro is chewy and tender.
3. Drain the excess liquid from the farro and set aside the farro.
4. While the farro is cooking, wash and dry the kale leaves.
5. Stack several leaves on top of each other and slice off the few inches of tough, fibrous stem from the bottoms. If desired, slice out the ribs (though I like the crunch these ribs add to the salad).
6. Roughly chop the kale leaves into bite-sized pieces. Repeat stacking and slicing the remaining leaves of kale.
7. Transfer the chopped kale to a big mixing bowl. Whisk together the olive oil, miso paste, and lemon juice; pour over the kale leaves.
8. Use your hands to work the dressing into the kale leaves. Continue massaging the leaves until the kale has softened and feels silky, 1 to 2 minutes.

9. Pour the farro and the drained chickpeas over the kale and toss to combine. Taste and add a sprinkle of salt or another squeeze of lemon if desired.

10. Salad will keep in a covered container in the fridge for several days.

Apple Sandwiches With Almond Butter and Granola

Serves: 2   Calories: 90

Preparation Time: 5 minutes

Ingredients

- 1 apple, cored and sliced into rings
- Almond butter
- Granola

Method

1. Generously spread almond butter on one apple slice.
2. Sprinkle granola over almond butter and top with another apple slice.
3. Repeat using remaining apple slices and almond butter.

Avocado Tea Sandwiches

Serves: 1   Calories: 147

Preparation Time: 10 minutes

Ingredients

- 1 avocado, ripe, sliced
- 1 tablespoon reduced-fat mayonnaise
- ½ teaspoon lemon juice
- ⅛ teaspoon cracked black pepper
- 8 very thin slices wheat bread
- 2 ounces thinly sliced smoked salmon
- 12 thin slices European cucumber

Method

1. Combine mayonnaise, lemon juice and pepper in a small bowl.
2. Thinly spread on bread and top with salmon, avocado and cucumber.

Hummus and Veggie Sandwich

Serves: 1 Calories: 336

Preparation Time: 10 minutes

Ingredients

- 2 slices of sprouted whole-grain bread
- 2 tablespoons hummus
- 3 thin slices of cucumber
- 2 thin slices of tomato
- 3 slices of avocado
- 1/4 cup alfalfa sprouts
- 1/4 cup grated carrots

Method

1. Toast your bread.
2. Spread one tablespoon of hummus on each slice of bread, layer up your veggies, and enjoy!

Pear-Walnut Sandwich

Serves: 4 Calories: 335

Preparation Time: 15 minutes

Ingredients

- 1/2 cup (4 ounces) tub-style light cream cheese
- 8 (1.1-ounce) slices cinnamon-raisin bread, toasted
- 2 tablespoons finely chopped walnuts, toasted
- 2 Bartlett pears, cored and thinly sliced
- 1 cup alfalfa sprouts

Method

1. Spread 1 tablespoon cream cheese evenly over each of 8 bread slices.
2. Sprinkle 1/2 tablespoon walnuts evenly over each of 4 bread slices.
3. Top each evenly with pear slices, sprouts, and 1 bread slice.
4. Cut each sandwich in half diagonally.

Turkey, Smashed Peas, and Pesto Sandwich

Serves: 4 Calories: 459

Preparation Time: 15 minutes

Ingredients

- 1/4 small red onion, sliced
- 2 tablespoons white wine vinegar
- 2 tablespoons butter
- 10 ounces frozen peas kosher salt and black pepper
- 1/4 cup pesto
- 8 ounces sliced roasted turkey
- 8 slices white country bread, toasted

Method

1. Toss the onion and vinegar in a small bowl. Let sit until the onion is tender and bright pink, 3 to 5 minutes.
2. Meanwhile, heat the butter in a medium skillet over medium heat.
3. Add the peas and ¼ teaspoon each salt and pepper and cook until heated through, 5 to 7 minutes. Mash until the peas hold together.
4. Divide the peas, onion, pesto, and turkey among the bread.

Lentils with Wine-Glazed Winter Vegetables

Serves: 4 Calories: 416

Preparation Time: 45 minutes

Ingredients

- 3 cups water
- 1 1/2 cups dried lentils
- 1 teaspoon salt, divided
- 1 bay leaf
- 1 1/2 teaspoons olive oil
- 2 cups chopped onion
- 1 1/2 cups chopped peeled celeriac (celery root)
- 1 cup diced parsnip
- 1 cup diced carrot
- 1 tablespoon minced fresh or 1 teaspoon dried tarragon, divided
- 1 tablespoon tomato paste
- 1 garlic clove, minced
- 2/3 cup dry red wine
- 2 teaspoons Dijon mustard
- 1 tablespoon butter
- 1/4 teaspoon black pepper

Method

1. Combine water, lentils, 1/2 teaspoon salt, and bay leaf in a medium saucepan; bring to a boil. Reduce heat, and simmer 25 minutes. Remove lentils from heat, and set aside.
2. Heat olive oil in a medium cast-iron or nonstick skillet over medium-high heat. Add the onion, celeriac, parsnip, carrot, and 1 1/2 teaspoons tarragon, and cook 10 minutes or until browned. Stir in 1/2 teaspoon salt, tomato paste, and garlic; cook mixture 1 minute. Stir in wine, scraping pan to loosen

browned bits. Bring to a boil; cover, reduce heat, and simmer 10 minutes or until vegetables are tender.

3. Stir in mustard. Add lentil mixture, and cook 2 minutes. Remove from heat; discard bay leaf, and stir in butter, 1 1/2 teaspoons tarragon, and pepper.

Honey-Roasted Root Vegetables

Serves: 4 Calories: 118

Preparation Time: 35 minutes

Ingredients

- 2 cups coarsely chopped peeled sweet potato (about 1 large)
- 1 1/2 cups coarsely chopped peeled turnip (about 2 medium)
- 1 1/2 cups coarsely chopped parsnip (about 2 medium)
- 1 1/2 cups coarsely chopped carrot (about 2 medium)
- 1/4 cup tupelo honey
- 2 tablespoons olive oil
- 1/2 teaspoon salt
- 3 shallots, halved Cooking spray

Method

1. Preheat oven to 450F/230C.
2. Combine all ingredients except the cooking spray in a large bowl; toss to coat.
3. Place vegetable mixture on a jelly-roll pan coated with cooking spray.
4. Bake at 450F/230C for 35 minutes or until vegetables are tender and begin to brown, stirring every 15 minutes.
5. Pack the ingredients in a lunch box.

8. Pre-WORKOUT Meals and Snacks

Nutrition is a vital part of exercise and fitness, of course – it's pretty well known that what you eat plays a huge role in your health and overall fitness! But the specifics of exactly what to eat to get the most out of your exercise routine can be a little more confusing at sometimes. Are carbs good or bad? Should you be focusing on protein? And where does glucose come from it all?

In fact, there are no really 'bad' food groups – your body needs protein as well as some carbs in order to fuel it and get the most out of a workout, and sugar will provide you with the energy you need to power through. The trick is to make sure you're eating the right kinds and quantities of these food groups to fit in with what you're doing. Low-GI carbs which release sugar more slowly into the bloodstream will help you keep going far better than refined sugar or simpler carbs like white bread.

It's always a good idea to make sure you eat something before a workout; either a larger meal a few hours beforehand, or a light snack an hour or two before you start. The closer to your workout you eat, the smaller and more carb-focused your food should be – if you've only got an hour, try some cereal or something light and vegetable-based.

Eating during exercise is also an option; while it's generally considered less vital than eating beforehand, some people find that snacking on small, portable treats like energy balls improve their stamina and their workout experience in general. Of course, if you're going to be doing prolonged exercise such as a long hike, it's important to make sure you eat throughout the day – bring something you can wrap up and keep in a backpack that will give you enough energy to keep going! And of course, with any kind of exercise, it's vital to stay hydrated – make sure you've always got that water bottle within reach. Power drinks or shakes can also be a good option!

After exercise, it's just as important to make sure you eat within a couple of hours. A combination of carbs and protein will help to rebuild muscle proteins, cutting down on that sore feeling the next day, and will boost your energy back up so you can get on with the rest of the day. Research suggests that eating shortly after a workout is the best option – after just two hours or so the benefits will decrease, so it's a good idea to prepare something in advance, or choose something that's quick and easy to put together.

The recipes in this book generally offer a combination of protein and slow-release carbs, with some sugar here and there for taste and a quick energy boost. They range from very low in calories too much heartier meals to pick you up after a tough workout and keep you going – so there should be something here for almost every occasion!

Energy Balls

Serves: makes 8 balls

Calories: approx 120 per ball

Preparation Time: 20 minutes

Ingredients

- 2 scoops protein powder
- 4 tbsp peanut butter
- 4 tbsp maple syrup or honey
- Chopped nuts, grated coconut, chocolate chips, oatmeal, or any other toppings you like

Method

1. Mix together the protein powder, honey or syrup, and peanut butter, in a bowl. Stir very thoroughly until everything is mixed together fairly smoothly.
2. Add any toppings you want.
3. Roll the mixture into balls using your hands.
4. Eat immediately, or refrigerate until you need them!

Almond Quinoa Porridge

Serves: 1-2   Calories: 545

Preparation Time: 20 minutes

Ingredients

- ½ cup quinoa
- 2 cups almond milk
- 1 banana or a handful of blueberries
- 1 tbsp flaked almonds
- 1 tsp ground cinnamon (optional)

Method

1. Put the quinoa and almond milk into a saucepan and bring to the boil.
2. Reduce the heat and simmer for around 10 minutes.
3. Stir in the cinnamon (if using).
4. Simmer for another 5 minutes or until the liquid is mostly absorbed and the quinoa reaches the consistency you prefer.
5. Slice the banana.
6. Serve the porridge in a bowl and top with almonds and sliced banana or blueberries.

Peanut Butter Banana Toast

Serves: 1   Calories: 470

Preparation Time: 15 minutes

Ingredients

- 2 slices wholemeal bread
- 2 tbsp peanut butter
- 1 large banana
- 1 tsp honey (optional)

Method

1. Lightly toast the bread until it's golden brown.
2. Slice the banana into thin pieces.
3. Spread the peanut butter onto the toast.
4. Top with the banana and, if you wish, drizzle a little honey over the top. Eat immediately.

Strawberry Cottage Cheese Parfait

Serves: 1   Calories: approx 145

Preparation Time: 10 minutes

Ingredients

- ½ cup fresh strawberries
- ½ cup cottage cheese
- 2 tbsp unflavoured Greek or plain yogurt
- 1 tsp chopped walnuts or a handful of rolled oats (optional)

Method

1. Slice or roughly chop the strawberries and put to one side.
2. Mix together the cottage cheese and yogurt.
3. Add the strawberries to a cup or glass, reserving about 1 tbsp.
4. Spoon the cottage cheese/yogurt mixture over the strawberries.
5. Top with the remaining strawberries and walnuts or oats.
6. Eat immediately.

Scrambled Eggs with Cheese

Serves: 1   Calories: 290

Preparation Time: 10 minutes

Ingredients

- 2 large eggs
- ¼ cup shredded or grated Cheddar cheese
- ½ tsp butter or oil
- Pinch of salt
- Pinch of black pepper
- Splash of milk (optional)

Method

1. Break the eggs into a large bowl and whisk until the egg yolks and whites are thoroughly mixed.
2. Stir the salt, pepper, milk and cheese through the mixture.
3. Heat up a frying pan with a little oil and pour in the egg mixture.
4. Stir as the egg cooks until it reaches the consistency you prefer.
5. Serve and eat immediately.

Hazelnut Broccoli Salad

Serves: 1   Calories: approx 700

Preparation Time: 15 minutes

Ingredients

- ½ cup hazelnuts, shelled and halved
- 1 cup broccoli
- ½ cup crumbled feta cheese
- ½ cup cherry tomatoes
- 1 tsp olive oil
- 1 tsp lemon juice

Method

1. Break or chop the broccoli into small florets.
2. Boil or steam the broccoli until it's bright green and just starting to soften, but still crunchy (boil for around 1 minute or steam for 2).
3. Drain the broccoli and allow to cool.
4. Halve the cherry tomatoes.
5. Mix together the broccoli, tomatoes, feta and hazelnuts.
6. Stir through the olive oil and lemon juice.
7. Serve immediately or refrigerate.

Tuna Apple Salad

Serves: 1   Calories: 540

Preparation Time: 10 minutes

Ingredients

- 1 tin tuna
- 1 apple
- 1 stalk of celery
- ½ cup sweetcorn
- 2 tbsp mayonnaise
- Handful of lettuce leaves
- Pinch of salt or garlic salt

Method

1. Drain the tuna and place into a large bowl.
2. Dice the apple and celery.
3. Mix together the tuna, sweetcorn, apple, celery, salt and mayonnaise. Stir well.
4. Serve with the lettuce and eat immediately.

Honey Nut Apples

Serves: 1   Calories: approx 600

Preparation Time: 10 minutes

Ingredients

- 1 large apple
- 2 tbsp nut butter (almond, peanut or whatever you prefer)
- 1 tbsp honey
- 1 banana
- 1 scoop protein powder
- 1 tbsp cocoa powder (optional)

Method

1. Mash the banana in a bowl.
2. Combine the mashed banana, nut butter, honey, protein powder and cocoa powder and stir thoroughly until fairly smooth.
3. Slice the apple.
4. Spread the honey-nut spread onto apple slices.
5. Eat immediately or refrigerate for later.

Lentil Salad

Serves: 1   Calories: approx 160

Preparation Time: 2-3 hours

Ingredients

- ¼ cup brown lentils
- ¼ tin black beans
- 1 red or yellow bell pepper
- ¼ red onion or 1 green onion
- 1 stalk celery
- 1 tsp cilantro, chopped (optional)
- 1 tsp olive oil
- 1 tsp lemon juice
- 1 tsp paprika

Method

1. Place lentils into a small saucepan, cover with water, bring to the boil and simmer for 30-40 minutes until they're tender and cooked through.
2. Drain the lentils and allow to cool.
3. Rinse the beans in a colander with cold water and dry with paper towels.
4. Dice the onion, bell pepper and celery.
5. Mix together the lentils, beans, bell pepper, onion and celery.
6. Stir through the olive oil, paprika and lemon/lime juice.
7. Refrigerate for at least an hour or two to let the flavours mingle.

Egg White Omelette

Serves: 1   Calories: 160

Preparation Time: 20 minutes

Ingredients

- 3 eggs
- 1 cup fresh spinach leaves
- 1 tbsp water
- 1 tomato
- 2 tbsp cottage cheese
- 1 tsp butter or oil

Method

1. Separate the egg whites and reserve the yolks for future use.
2. Whisk together the egg whites and water in a bowl.
3. Dice the tomato and shred the spinach leaves.
4. Heat the oil in a skillet, then add the tomato and spinach and allow the spinach leaves to wilt for a minute.
5. Pour in the egg whites and stir through.
6. Cook until the egg whites are almost set. Use a spoon or spatula to lift up the edges and let any uncooked whites run underneath to cook.
7. Spoon the cottage cheese into the middle of the omelette.
8. Fold over the omelette edges to wrap around the cheese.
9. Serve immediately.

Greek Yogurt Cup

Serves: 1   Calories: 370

Preparation Time: 5 minutes

Ingredients

- ¾ cup plain Greek yogurt
- 2 tbsp granola
- ½ banana
- 2 tbsp blueberries

Method

1. Finely slice the banana.
2. Pour the Greek yogurt into a bowl or glass.
3. Stir the granola through it.
4. Top with the banana and blueberries.
5. Eat immediately or refrigerate for an hour or two until needed.

Homemade Chocolate Protein Bites

Serves: Makes 4-8 bars

Calories: 160-290 per bar depending on size

Preparation Time: 45 minutes

Ingredients

- ½ cup almond or peanut butter
- 1 ½ tbsp almond milk or soy milk
- 2 tbsp brown rice syup
- 1 tbsp cocoa powder
- 2 tbsp protein powder
- ¼ cup rolled oats
- Handful of chocolate chips and/or raisins

Method

1. Mix together the nut butter, almond/soy milk and syrup in a large bowl.
2. Stir in the protein powder, cocoa powder, oats and chocolate chips/raisins and mix thoroughly until the mixture is smooth and feels like cookie dough.
3. Line a baking tray with parchment paper and spread the dough into it in a thick, even layer. Refrigerate for 30 minutes.
4. Slice into squares or bars.
5. Eat immediately, or refrigerate/freeze for later.

Avocado and Eggs

Serves: 1   Calories: approx 350

Preparation Time: 15 minutes

Ingredients

- 1 large avocado
- 1 egg
- 1 tsp lemon juice
- Pinch of salt
- 1 tbsp mayonnaise or salad dressing (optional)

Method

1. Boil the egg for approximately 10 minutes, or until it's at your preferred consistency (but make sure the white is solid).
2. Slice the avocado in half and remove the stone.
3. Sprinkle the lemon juice over the avocado.
4. Slice the boiled egg in half.
5. Nestle each half-egg into the hole left by the avocado stone.
6. Dress with mayonnaise or salad dressing if desired.
7. Eat immediately.

Cottage Cheese Bowl

Serves: 1   Calories: approx 350

Preparation Time: 5 minutes

Ingredients

- 1 cup cottage cheese
- ½ cup walnuts
- ¼ cup raisins (optional)
- Pinch of cinnamon (optional)

Method

1. Crush the walnuts until they're in fairly small pieces.
2. Put the cottage cheese into a bowl.
3. Mix the raisins (if using) through the cottage cheese.
4. Top with crushed walnuts and (if using) cinnamon.
5. Serve and eat immediately.

9. Desserts

Mug Brownies

Serves: 1   Calories: approx. 300

Preparation Time: 10 minutes

Ingredients

- 4 tbsp. flour
- 2 tbsp. cocoa powder
- 2 tbsp. white sugar
- 2 tbsp. water or milk
- 2 tbsp. oil or melted butter
- ¼ tsp vanilla essence (optional)
- Pinch of salt
- Chocolate chips, mini marshmallows, any other toppings you like

Method

1. Mix together the dry ingredients in a coffee mug.
2. Stir in the water (or milk) and oil (or softened butter) and mix it all up until the mixture forms a smooth, thick paste. You can add a little more liquid here for a softer, gooier brownie if you like.
3. Microwave on high, for one minute. (Be careful when removing the mug as it may be hot!)
4. Sprinkle with chocolate chips and/or marshmallows and serve immediately – you can eat it straight from the mug, or scoop it out and serve it up on a plate with ice-cream.

Chocolate Mousse

Serves: 4   Calories: approx 450 per serving

Preparation Time: 2-3 hours

Ingredients

- 200g (14oz) dark or milk chocolate
- ½ cup water
- 3 eggs
- 1/3 cup sugar
- Whipped cream/chopped nuts/chocolate sprinkles or any other toppings you like, to serve

Method

1. Break up the chocolate into small chunks – kids can do this, first breaking it up with their hands and then breaking the smaller pieces with a rolling pin.
2. Heat up a pan of water over a low heat until it's just simmering, then place a heatproof bowl over the top of it. Add the half-cup of water to the bowl and let it warm up for a minute before adding the chocolate.
3. Heat up the chocolate until it melts, stirring it regularly. Ask children to keep an eye on it and check how soft and melted it's getting.
4. When the chocolate is melted thoroughly, take it off the heat and let it cool for two to three minutes.
5. Separate the eggs. You can show children how to do this using the two halves of the eggshell, a spoon or even their fingers (cup the yolk in their hands and let the white trickle through their fingers – a little messy but effective and fun!).
6. When the chocolate has cooled slightly, stir the egg yolks into it and mix well.
7. Add the egg whites to a clean bowl, then whisk them until they begin to form soft peaks. Once they do, whisk in the sugar a little at a time, making sure it's thoroughly whisked in until the mixture looks glossy.

8. Using a spoon, very gently fold the egg-white mixture into the chocolate. Make sure you do this lightly to keep the air and lightness of the mousse.
9. Put the chocolate mousse into the fridge to chill for at least two hours. You can separate it into individual serving bowls or glasses first if you wish as it will set a little.
10. Serve with whipped cream, a few sprinkles and any other toppings you want – again, kids can choose their ingredients and do this part themselves!

Fresh Blackberry Pie

Serves: 4   Calories: 426

Preparation Time: 55 minutes

Ingredients

- 1 cup sugar
- 1/3 cup quick-cooking tapioca
- 4 cups fresh blackberries, divided
- 2 tablespoons butter
- Pastry for double-crust pie (9 inches)

Method

1. In a large saucepan, combine the sugar, tapioca and salt. Add 1 cup blackberries; toss to coat. Let stand for 15 minutes.
2. Cook and stir over medium heat until berries burst and mixture comes to a gentle boil. Remove from the heat; gently stir in remaining berries.
3. Line a 9-in. Pie plate with bottom pastry; trim pastry even with edge of plate. Add filling; dot with butter. Roll out remaining pastry to fit top of pie; place over filling. Trim, seal and flute edges. Cut slits in top.
4. Bake at 400F/205C for 35-40 minutes or until crust is golden brown and filling is bubbly. Cool on a wire rack.

Peanut Butter Cup Trifle

Serves: 4   Calories: 250

Preparation Time: 20 minutes

Ingredients

- 4 cups cold 2% milk
- 2 packages (3.9 ounces each) instant chocolate pudding mix
- 1 prepared angel food cake (8 to 10 ounces), cut into 1-inch cubes
- 1 carton (12 ounces) frozen whipped topping, thawed
- 2 packages (8 ounces each) Reese's mini peanut butter cups

Method

1. In a large bowl, whisk milk and pudding mixes 2 minutes. Let stand 2 minutes or until soft-set.
2. In a 3-qt. trifle bowl or glass bowl, layer half of the cake cubes, pudding, whipped topping and peanut butter cups. Repeat layers.
3. Refrigerate for atleast 15 minutes until serving.

Strawberry-Rosemary Yogurt Pops

Serves: 4   Calories: 80

Preparation Time: 30 minutes

Ingredients

- 1 cup chopped fresh strawberries
- 2 tablespoons strawberry preserves
- 2 fresh rosemary sprigs
- 1-1/2 cups (12 ounces) vanilla yogurt
- 6 freezer pop molds or paper cups (3 ounces each) and wooden pop or lollipop sticks

Method

1. In a small bowl, mix strawberries, vinegar, preserves and rosemary.
2. Let stand 30 minutes; discard rosemary.
3. Spoon 2 tablespoons yogurt and 1 tablespoon strawberry mixture into each mold or paper cup. Repeat layers.
4. Top molds with holders. If using cups, top with foil and insert sticks through foil. Freeze until firm.

Easy Cake Mix Bars

Serves: 4 Calories: 113

Preparation Time: 20 minutes

Ingredients

- 1 yellow cake mix (regular size)
- 1 large egg
- 1/2 cup 2% milk
- 1/3 cup canola oil
- 1 cup white baking chips and jimmies

Method

1. Preheat oven to 350F/175C. In a large bowl, combine cake mix, egg, milk and oil (mixture will be thick). Stir in baking chips and jimmies. Spread into a greased 15x10x1-in. Baking pan.
2. Bake 18-20 minutes or until a toothpick inserted in center comes out clean. Cool completely in pan on a wire rack. Cut into bars.
3. Freeze option: Freeze bars in freezer containers. To use, thaw in covered containers before serving.

Ice Cream Kolachkes

Serves: 4   Calories: 61

Preparation Time: 20 minutes

Ingredients

- 2 cups butter, softened
- 1-pint vanilla ice cream, softened
- 4 cups all-purpose flour
- 2 tablespoons sugar
- 2 cans (12 ounces each) apricot and/or raspberry cake and pastry filling

Method

1. In the bowl of a heavy-duty stand mixer, beat butter and ice cream until blended (mixture will appear curdled).
2. Add flour and sugar; mix well. Divide dough into four portions; cover and refrigerate 2 hours or until easy to handle.
3. Preheat oven to 350F/175C. On a lightly floured surface, roll one portion of dough into a 12x10–in. Rectangle; cut into 2-in. Squares.
4. Place a teaspoonful of filling in the center of each square. Overlap two opposite corners of dough over filling; pinch tightly to seal.
5. Place 2 in. Apart on ungreased baking sheets. Repeat with remaining dough and filling.
6. Bake 11-14 minutes or until bottoms are lightly browned. Cool 1 minute before removing from pans to wire racks.
7. Sprinkle with confectioners' sugar if desired.

The recipe for a joyful life!

Serves: *all your family*

Cooking Time: *a few minutes every day*

Ingredients

- good mood
- positive thinking

Directions

- *Make small surprises for your loved ones*
- *Do charity work*
- *More often do your favorite thing*
- *Spend more time with children and the elderly*
- *Go in for sports*
- *Read books*
- *Learn the languages*
- *More walking*
- *Do exercises*
- *Throw away unnecessary things from home*
- *Plan an interesting weekend*
- *Take photos*
- *Smile more often*
- *Hug your loved ones*
- *Meditate*

YOUR FREE GIFT

I wanted to show my appreciation that you support my work so I've put together a free gift for you.

Take your Free Bonus here

Just visit the link above to download it now.

I know you will love this gift.

Thank you for attention!

With love,

Tim Gray

www.ingramcontent.com/pod-product-compliance
Lightning Source LLC
Chambersburg PA
CBHW081737220526

45468CB00008B/2139